Spirit Eyes

Also by Maurice Whelan

Non-fiction

Special Education and Social Control: Invisible Disasters
Mistress of Her Own Thoughts: Ella Freeman Sharpe
In the Company of William Hazlitt

Fiction published by Ginninderra Press
Boat People

Poetry published by Ginninderra Press
The Lilac Bow
Excalibur's Return
A Season and a Time

Maurice Whelan

Spirit Eyes

Acknowledgements

My thanks to those who read and comment on my work:
Lena Bruselid, Michael Dudley, Winton Higgins, Elaine Kelly,
Catherine Hickey, Richard O'Neill-Dean, Lorraine Rose,
Louise Whelan.

My continuing thanks to Stephen Matthews
for publishing my work.

Dedicated to May Gibson

Spirit Eyes
ISBN 978 1 76041 288 3
Copyright © text Maurice Whelan 2017
Cover photo © Maurice Whelan

First published 2017 by
Ginninderra Press
PO Box 3461 Port Adelaide 5015 Australia
www.ginninderrapress.com.au

Contents

Sightings	7
With Spirit Eyes	11
Together Again	12
Breaking the Sound Barrier	13
A Dance	14
The Years Were Counted	15
The Relay	16
Changing of the Guard	17
Movement in the Clouds	18
The Painter	19
Fringe Dweller	20
Sightings in the USA	21
Beside Oneself	24
The Two of Us	26
Is That You	27
Morning Glory	28
Going Back	29
Smell the Roses	30
Zero?	31
Advanced At Speed	32
The Load	33
Gifts	34
Among Trees	42
Snap	43
The Fall	44
Japanese Gardens	45
Imitating Art	46
An Olive Grove	47
Coral Bay WA	48
Chatswood NSW	49

Rise Up	50
The Bougainvillea and Calliandra	51
I Think Better in the Dark	52
Silence Streams	53
Yours Sincerely	54
I, George Scrivens	55
At Ullamalla	57
Hymn for Heaney	58
Old Ground	59

Sightings

Like lakes, like rivers,
The poet's stance
Sometimes is still,
Sometimes shimmers.

At Haguro-san in Japan's snow mountains it is quiet,
And the annals say, spirits move inside each snow flake.
Amaterasu, the sun god saw the dancing shades of white,
Streamed life and light into the mountain lake.
In the Heian dynasty bronze-smiths cast mirrors adorned
With cranes, and believing the polished metal held their visage,
People placed mirrors in Amaterasu's lake, to be with her,
To share long life, to be at one with flakes of light.
Fast forward time. Bridge builders drain the lake,
And find six hundred mirrors from the dynasty of Heian.
To the old smiths' craft the world's once more awake,
And magic mirrors mould the face of man.
In books and museums, we, the gods of light may know.
One day to Haguro-san I'll go; I'm drawn to flakes of snow.

Among the many moments that comprised his years,
One was, he said, supreme, exalted, made him whole;
A portal to an inner world was opened wide by tears,
Hazel eyes revealed to him rich secrets of the soul.
She, a face in the crowd moved one way, he the other.
Tear-filled eyes through him and from him
Sought salvation, sought release from shame;
Without a word he freed her of all blame.
He never saw her again; there was no before or after.

Daily, within his now crowded world she comes,
Visitation he knows for sure will never cease:
Tearful Vermeer girl with pearl earring – his masterpiece.
Through eyes' windows he saw, and he was seen,
Fate, he said, had honoured him, a humble human being.

Sometimes it seems the soul's so vast,
Streaming on its path from day of birth,
Fine-woven from invisible threads to last,
From babe's first cry until the hour of death.
Sometimes to me it seems, once born
Imagination, gazelle-like moves in bounds,
Journeys, like prayer, without fear of scorn,
Through silent worlds in search of distant sounds.
Sometimes, ourselves we strive to teach.
Fate's more powerful and can trump design,
What's most glorious is always out of reach,
Like life itself: a mystery, gifted and benign.
On a well-greased weighbridge, we balance all our being,
One glance made glorious; all else by us unseen.

She rose from her straight-backed chair
The moment he released his final breath.
A sigh. A single audible intake of air.
One lives on, the other gone to death.
And now the silence faintly fractures,
A pitter-patter of small steps move from
Room to room, upstairs and down, she covers wall
Mirrors with veils, free-standers laid face-down-flat.

No more will my eyes in his be shown,
Where all my life myself I've seen,
Where all my life myself I've known,
Therein, I, wordless love did glean.
A clock strikes thrice; I have to let him go.
Time speeding on; time reversing slow.

An early autumn morning rise. 'It's mushroom time,'
A whisper in my ear, 'let's surprise the sun.'
Pants pulled up, shirt cuffs down, buttons all align.
I'm lifted and lowered into waiting boots. 'We're on.'
In a green-grass field we stood at break of day,
Misty breaths like young clouds met and mingled.
Large hands rubbed small to keep the early chill at bay,
While mosque-like domes of white emerged perfected.
On our spider-web sea – like a ship's fine-fibred
Rigging laced with sparkling diamonds –
Dew drops glisten. Heaven's silence breaks;
Corncrakes' crek-crek calls clatter in the crisp air.
The beauty of this world was then to me revealed,
And so forever my heart's love of life was sealed.

She's back dressed in widow's black.
Forehead, eyes and cheeks by veil obscured.
White handkerchief knotted in white-knuckled hand.
In the straight-backed chair she sits, her lips
As his, still. Can I hear a voice within the quiet?
Is it a song or string music wafting in?

The melody in my bone-marrow is known,
And to Amaterasu's mirrors my mind has flown.
Like flocks of cranes that merge in luscious white
Our spirits rise and float through flakes of light.
Through Haguro-san's hills and lake of life we drift.
How can one death bloom with peace so bright?
Some stare perpetual at tomorrow's crystal ball.
To the present moment, now, I give my all.

'Fret not when my leave I take of you
Let memory's magic wait for my return,
Light that lit our path was of an altered hue
And time then measured by a different sun.
Footprints in old woods where we did walk,
A lark ascending, a swooping goshawk,
The taste of berries red and blue – all hold fast
To echo seasons long since drifted past.
The scudding clouds, escarpments steep,
Crimson sunsets, oceans wide and deep
Mesmerised me. You leaned to the near and small:
Dew drops, fire flies, dust motes – jewels all.'
All nature and your eyes together mirrored me;
Taught me what I was, who I ought to be.

With Spirit Eyes

The stance is upright,
the walk straight and strong.
'Cuts a fine figure,' you might remark.

Until you look with spirit eyes;

like a tree whose roots years past
have suffered a seismic shift,
he leans north by north-west.

His stare interrogates
the red sunset, the pink sunrise,
and lush green fields beyond.

He strains into his tomorrow,
tomorrow where his today is lived;

all present scents, sights and songs
vacancies unfilled.

Together Again

If I say I, or me, or mine,
I wish, I want, I will, I won't,
I think, I feel, or I say
Once upon a time I

Did this or that, take heed.
Because an I is prone to
Wander into another
I, and become if truth

Be told alike to you.
And following in your
Shadow – be you old
Or child, tame or wild –

Bending to your line of
Light the poet begins
To carve, to chisel,
To polish words,

That move and breathe.
And when the poem
Is done and serves
Your I as mirror, I

Beg pardon, must dispose
Of ye, to backward glance,
On second sights to see
Those hidden parts of me.

Breaking the Sound Barrier

My ears do seek the sound I hold most dear
And keep it softly deep inside my heart,
But my lips fail to shape the words I hear
And speech defeats me as a living art.
My childhood friends would shout and call,
The world they learned to know by name,
Like mountain streams their words would fall:
Would seek and find; would wildness tame.
I learned to write. On an anvil I forged
Words, white hot; so hot their fury stormed.
Words soft, so soft their silence screamed,
Through galaxies my mute voice beamed.
Unmute me. Gift your lips. Lest my spirit wane
Strike my flinted words, set my heart aflame.

A Dance

Music is stupendous; it sets the heart on fire,
Feet and fingers tap; we clap and shout encore.
But poems' silent songs are my soul's deep desire.

The multitude of voices from instruments and choir,
Unity and diversity, harmony and dissonance explore.
Music is stupendous; it sets the heart on fire.

Yeats said, 'Come from the holy fire, perne in a gyre
And be the singing-masters of my soul,' and more.
Poems' silent songs were his soul's deep desire.

Viola, violin, bass and cello assemble and aspire
To speak the speechless from our deepest core.
Music is stupendous; it sets the heart on fire.

When next you read a poem listen for the lyre
And words by fingers plucked. And ask it of your
Self – are silent songs your soul's deep desire?

Wordless music, musical words; we dance upon a wire.
Spread wings, trust words with silent strings and soar.
Music is stupendous; it sets our hearts on fire.
And poems' silent songs sing our soul's deep desire.

The Years Were Counted

The years were counted
As they passed,
So too the days and weeks
And months measured.

And still it came
As a surprise
To be called old,
And there was wonder –
Where did the years go?
You'd need eyes
In the back of your head
To keep track of it all.

The Relay

'Hold on now.
Not so tight.'

The feeble fingers
Relaxed their grip.

'Best held with ease
And carried lightly.

Do your part.
Hand it on.'

Changing of the Guard

A changing of the guard, a sultry summer day,
His fruitful labour, progress deems now past,
A man of his time, his time had sped away.

He ploughed with horses, with scythe he cut the hay,
His harvest fields of sheaves would not outlast
A changing of the guard. One sultry summer day

I saw him stoop, the burdens of the new weigh
Heavy, his tearless sorrow deep and vast.
A man of his time, his time had sped away.

My fifty sowings and fifty harvests I survey,
The times rolled on, moved forward. Oh so fast
A changing of the guard; a sultry summer day.

Care For The Land – the call I did obey,
And like old Danny, faithful to the last;
Men of our time, our times now speed away.

My loft's rich store of memory each day I assay,
And garner stillness – it is a potent yeast.
A changing of the guard, a sultry summer day,
A man in my time; time not yet sped away.

Movement in the Clouds

Movement in the clouds
And on the sea stilled

As she approached. Her presence
Like a magnetic force drew us near.

Her size belied the strength inside
That fragile frame, and like a slow

Moving stream her words flowed
Soft and free, her ease infectious.

The Painter

Lost in her own stare
The silent land was all

Breeze-waves
On grass, on corn,

Swooping peregrine,
Rising waterfowl,

All stilled in that
Contracted stare,

In watercolour framed,
Pronounced eternal.

Fringe Dweller

Staffs of life
Are to her abhorrent.

With unwavering gaze
And resolute lips

With hollow cheeks
And shrunken limbs

To numb her gnawing
Need she strides

With flailing arms
A moving crucifixion.

Sightings in the USA

Portland, Oregon

Tree at lake's edge fallen.
Branches bend to touch.
Moonlight mirrors white.

Silvered roof tops,
wintered cedar trees –
house sprouts green.

In the walled stone
garden no flowers grow –
light grows luminous.

Branches overhang
silver pond
ornate mirror to the sky.

Martha's Vineyard, Massachusetts

Hardy tubers
break the earth –
Mount Everest rises.

Grey wooden jetties
pointed masts pierce
monochrome sky –

Raindrops on lake,
pebbles from heaven.
Circles collide.

New York City

Cherry blossom canopy,
carpet of petals –
Saturn's rings spin pink.

Times Square sidewalks,
stages to strut upon –
aliens pass unchecked.

Chatter everywhere –
why don't people
sing like birds?

Streets you knew to
find yourself upon –
Pluto in elliptical orbit.

Profiles pass
café window,
curious family album.

8 Spruce Street steel
twists and curves –
wintered branches.

St Paul's at Ground Zero,
grief clouds linger –
a poem is a flimsy thing.

Hudson River Pier stumps,
decayed dots of darkness –
sinking tombstones.

Beside Oneself

Alone on the dawn run
Following the river bank,
A night-like water mist
Wakes from heavy sleep.

Ghost from the deep
Entering the unwary,
An ague – or maybe
The river's soul.

Alone no more,
A throng of runners'
Steps and sweats and
Breaths match mine.

To live inside one's
Present or look back,
To forty years of runs,
Twenty on this river track.

Slower now; not so far to go.
Aloud, what beauty that
Mist holds, I say. As one
All nod and echo me.

*

More company awaits,
A goanna on a fallen tree.
Its small eyes
Wide and wondrous.

He leaps into the air,
With gravity defied
He hits the ground
With a thud. Before

The fall I saw the bird
In him, winged and light,
Reaching for tree tops,
And beyond, the stars.

The Two of Us

I marvel at my hand,
That holds the knife,
That dips into the honey,
That twists and lifts.

As if the child in me,
Who tried and tried again,
With pride in his mastery
Watches from within.

Well done. Did you hear?
A whisper. Yes. As real
As when first said and heard
And smiled upon.

Is That You

Knowing what the visit gave,
What I'd come away with,
What the days I spent

Back on the farm
All added up to,
Were incomplete,

Until yesterday when
I laughed out loud,
At something or other.

There you were, the timbre,
The threads of your voice
Were woven into mine

Echoing through the rooms
Of my home in Sydney.
Perfected counterpoint.

Morning Glory

As far as memory travelled
Breakfast time had been a time
Compacted. A space
Where remnants of past nights
Were gathered, dream kernels
Garnered and husks of night let
Flounder on the wind.

Going Back

for May Gibson (1918–

The last time we met you said
You were pleased I had come
On foot, that I had walked the
Mile or more from Shangana
To see you. And later when I
Bade goodbye you watched and
Waved and smiled as I resumed
My journey, to cross the fields,
To walk the road's green verge.
We had an hour. We talked of life.
We laughed. Were silent. Read poetry.
Tea and whiskey were had.

What was it about the walking?
Until I come again I'll wonder,
Was it that in these days
Of rush and speedy travel
My walking had rewound the
Clock of days and years
And we both returned in time
To times when people paused
To hear, to see, to smell, to touch
The world they're passing through,
Where that inner need for peace
And pace and calm is listened to?

Smell the Roses

They'll rush you, try to make you do as you are told:
Obey your elders; they know best, it's wise to behave.
Take time. Look at life as you would a flower unfold.

When the crowd cheers and you don't fit the mould
And they see you have it in you to be brave,
They'll rush you, try to make you do as you are told.

The rose, the tulip, the hyacinth and the marigold
Do not require you to be their master or their slave.
Take time. Look at life as you would a flower unfold.

Petals purple, orange, yellow, blue and gold
Are balm; will lap your body like a gentle wave.
They'll rush you, try to make you do as you are told

And may invoke the Bard – 'tides in the affairs', etc, old
Wisdom misused. You'll be mocked – they'll call you knave!
Take time. Look at life as you would a flower unfold.

The Mexican orchid blooms; with its scent your lungs implode.
Chocolate vanilla essence – nothing more your heart can crave.
Resist the rush. When they try to make you do as you are told
Take time. Look at life as you would a flower unfold.

Zero?

Zero is nought. Nothing from nothing springs.
What's made must have its maker, effect its cause,
Yet who can say from where creation sings?

We live by physics' laws, are drawn by nature's strings,
Science fiction's fiction – the grown-up's Santa Claus.
Zero is nought. Nothing from nothing springs.

The last in line digs deep and sprints and wins,
Is first to touch the tape to loud applause,
Now who can say from where creation sings?

To certainty in science mankind sternly clings,
Seeks sameness in what will be, what is and was.
Zero is nought. Nothing from nothing springs.

A poem comes from nought, from zero grows its wings.
Be brave, be swept into its slipstream because
You may learn from where creation sings?

On science's fertile ground do not fear the slings
Of wild imaginings. Become a wizard of Oz!
Zero is nought? Nothing from nothing springs?
Will you say from where creation sings?

Advanced At Speed

He advanced at speed, scattered
Everyone left, right and centre,
Ploughed his way through the crowd.

His horses and his chariot
Would with bladed wheels
Have mown down challengers.

With forward thrusting head,
Eyes so steely grey,
Twisted fingers grip the joystick

Of his electric wheelchair,
Pressing, propelling, embracing,
Embraced by the inexorable.

The Load

The load was back-breaking,
he brought in an earth mover
                      the size of a house.

Something smaller was needed,
A digger, a large shovel
                      a little spade.

Before I knew it he was down
On his knees, in his hand
                      a trowel.

Now the load is so small
He has to squint to see it.
                      That's enough.

A single moment,
The one you hold.
                      Enough.

Gifts

I find ecstasy in living;
The mere sense of living is joy enough.
– Emily Dickinson

The Gift of Being

To be,
Or never to have been,
Not how, or Who created
The simple fact of Being,
That the animate and inanimate
Are.

The Gift of Sound

In the beginning, drifting,
In water music, near-distant
Voices, sea sounds purred.
I, by spell am bound and
In murmurings turn and turn.

A scream launches me into
A world, into a universe of
Word and voice and song,
Nature's waves and crashing winds,
Whispering reeds and singing birds.

The Gift of Sight

What's dim and dark and light,
What is near and what is far is for me
To master, and when we change from night
To day, when a cloud moves slow or faster,
Which evening star shines first or last or
Snatches light from out our grasp as
Arrow speeds away from eye of archer.

The Gift of Smell

I, the most elusive sense,
Wayward in my innocence,
Beguiling in my secrecy,
Defy your words to capture me.

On musky scent of Jezebel
Kingdoms rose and kingdoms fell.
An ounce, a gram, a waft of me,
Drove men to conquer land and sea.

The Gift of Touch

Mine's the strangest sense of all
To heights I rise, to depths I fall.
Sometimes I'm moved by tender things
And in bliss I float as if on wings.
A finger stroke, a breath, a kiss
Can all the grief of life dismiss.
But when searing pain afflicts me
My deepest wish is not to be.

The Gift of Words

Before runic script and alphabets
Parchment and paper
Before man learned to write
It was all talk.

They were so in love with
Listening and some it must be said,
With the sound of their own voice,
It never occurred to anyone
To write it all down.

But seriously, I hear someone say,
Don't we have enough to read,
If we had all that our shelves
Would overflow, our libraries
Would be chock-a-block?

To which I say Amen, except,
If I can have the last word,
Wouldn't it be nice to know
What the first one was?

The Gift of Taste

Sometimes the thin slice,
The finely-cut portion
Outdoes the heavily-laden
Table; the wafer of fine
Cheese more satisfying
Than the full-blown meal.

A small memory in the
Shadows or angled light
Is sweeter than newfound
Praise and adulation.
So too the half-smile,
Walking side by side,
Reading together in silence,
Peaceful sleep savoured,
And quiet awakenings.

The Gift of Thought

If you imagine a triangle
Without angles, a square
Without sides,
You are close to
Apprehending a world
Without thought.

To think is so taken for granted
We presume its presence.
But if we try to perceive its
Absence we use it all the more.
Thinking is strongest when stretched.
No wonder our gods are all-knowing.

The Gift of Imagination

Can you compare me to a passing breeze,
Know I touch you but you can't say why?
On unmapped pathways do you move with ease,
And each day watch anew the eastern sky?
When reason can no longer be your guide
And will leads you to a sheer cliff face,
Do you sense my presence, at your side,
And that I offer gifts of human grace?
By day I move in fast-flowing streams,
Near touch and thought, near sound and sight;
At night I'm busy in the world of dreams,
Of stars, the moon my guiding light.
I have no name. One has called me Ariel.
In formless shadows I am known to dwell.

The Gift of Writing

It began with a lead pencil
And a crooked line
The teacher called diagonal.
It ended with a book, his name
Upon the dust cover.

He was taught to strive for
Sentences that rode the thermals,
Words that called like bugles
Or whispered softly in the ear.
Or in your steps stopped you still.

Someone said a pen can be
An artist's brush; you can paint,
Lay down shades of colour
Beyond the black and white.
So, as he did strive the child

Inside, tongue between teeth,
Hope riding high gripped
The pencil, pushed, prayed,
Implored the line –
Be straighter than the last.

Among Trees

If I was a tree and stood
Among blue gums and blackbutts
I would play host to
Sulphur-crested cockatoos
Kookaburras and currawongs
Butcher birds and magpies
Rainbow lorikeets and king parrots.
I would shimmer and tinkle
In a breeze.
When the wind raced
I'd sway and dance
And when at dawn
Their calls rang out
And the birds zigzagged
Through my foliage
I would conduct a symphony
And then when wind or
Breezeless evening came
By the sun's rich rays
My body would be painted
Pale-yellow and silver-grey
I'd watch my shadows stretch
And disappear to rest within
The quiet and silent night.

Snap

Beyond dense green trees
Lush apricot light,
Fierce, like fire
Ignites the skyscape.
Pink spokes pierce the foliage.

The sun is soon to set.
Like an awe-struck child
I snap my eyelids shut:
To defy the dying light;
To catch the vision bright.

The Fall

Some die a violent death,
uprooted in a storm,
or lose their place in the dead of night,
forsaken and forlorn.
This one's end was peaceful,
the fall quiet and slow,
the moon painted the heavens bright,
earth was all aglow.
I a privileged bystander,
away from the sleeping town,
saw its roots like a set of pulleys,
lever and lower it down.
It moved like an old clock's hand,
travelling from twelve to three,
touched the earth and hushed,
waves on a gentle sea.
As a child I sailed in its branches,
swung from the lowest bough,
its rustling words were magic,
balm to a fretful brow.
Each year on this night I return,
touch its now lichen-green prow,
remember the curtain descending,
grace in that slow final bow.

Japanese Gardens

Garden making is art, creates beauty to enthral,
Its elements earth, water, plant and stone,
And light, the most elusive but greatest power of all.

In Portland's garden colours cascade and fall,
Its rock and stone work raise you to a higher zone.
Garden making is art, creates beauty to enthral.

Brooklyn's pink petalled paths are nature's hall
Of fame. In your palm a blossom, sunbeams all your own:
Light, the most elusive but greatest power of all.

For hours I'd sit and watch, my back to the high wall
In Kildare's garden, Ireland – it became a second home.
Garden making is art, creates beauty to enthral.

I'd trace bonsai branch lines and the shadows of tall
Poplars. Water trickled, leaves changed their tone
With light, the most elusive but greatest power of all.

Plants offer peace when we listen to their call
To be with them in silence – you never walk alone.
Garden making is art, creates beauty to enthral.
Light, the most elusive and gentlest power of all.

Imitating Art

Like needles piercing silk
Pointed blackwood trees
Pierced the glass lake.

(A painted ship upon
A painted ocean
Sailed into view).

The leafless branches,
Brittle, silvered,
Seemed man-made

Structures. Thin bars
Of steel, protruding,
Sculptured, sparse.

An Olive Grove

for Peter Fullerton

It was the slope, the easy gradient
That caught the eye, invited focus.
A strip of land framed by trees
Trees framed by a strip of land,
Land and trees like lines on a
Draughtsman's page, signposts
To the man-made lake below.
All parts of the big picture.

So. When he tended root and branch
Cut and cleared, sprayed and picked –
Honourable manual labour – the
Big picture was in his grasp.
And when he laboured in that other
Place, sitting, listening, stretching
The sinews and muscles of his mind the
Big picture was in his grasp.

Like Faust he knew redemption
Comes through toil and reclamation.

Coral Bay WA

With outstretched arms
Face down we float,
Above a coral garden
Filled with liquid life.

Curves and lines below
Are strangely still. We hover
Above flowers in perpetual
Bloom, as if a master mason had

Chiselled them from rock their
Giant petals always open while
Small fish – some blue, some
Translucent – like bees above

Feed and tend their garden.
Our visiting time is brief,
This window into our past
Sea life fleeting. We glimpse

Far-distant seasons. This beauty
Is for eyes alone. No sound,
No breeze blown scent,
Not ever to be touched.

Chatswood NSW

There is a need for time alone
In gardens that are familiar
Among plants that are our own.
As I sit upon this bench
The thin grey veil of evening

Blends line and shape and curves
Past and present meld and
In memory I see rainbow light.
Flowers bloom, grevilleas glisten
Rosellas chatter, colours sway and dance.

An arm upon my shoulders.
The flowers remembered bloom
Again the colours dance.
Nature is our child and we
Her children and these trees

These shrubs, these flowers, this
Piece of earth, this patch of land,
The sun's rich rays are ours
To use, to borrow. And here
When tending time is spent

And thought extended
Our seasons move within.
Where truth and beauty calls
Labour is never priced
And love enthrals.

Rise Up

for St Mary's in Exile

A clean-skinned, flesh-coloured
Angophora stretched its limbs.
On its fingered extremities
A lorikeet lands. It sings.

I don't suppose it has any sense
Of privilege or knows I envy
It its call, its technicoloured coat,
Its vantage point, how it is free

To swoop; can make a perfect arc.
But I can imagine its wings being mine.
I rise, I swoop, I arc, I touch
The finger tips of the divine.

The Bougainvillea and Calliandra

The bougainvillea and calliandra
Grew side by side. The blooms
Of each in turn luxuriated.
Their upper, smaller branches
Dark and light, interlaced.
Nearer ground they chaffed,
Brushed against each other,
Tried to go their separate ways,
But their brushing and their chaffing
Gave way to braiding.
Intertwined, inseparable
They now share each other's sap.
To part would mean weeping
Wounds, torn white flesh,
Exposure to the elements.
Besides, the point at which
They've merged is the
Strongest point of all.

I Think Better in the Dark

I think better in the dark
When upon the other side of earth
The sun beams its heat and light
And people there awake and go
About their business
While here all but a few
Rest and sleep and dream.

There is strange comfort
When woken out of restless
Sleep from dreams that carry (fear
As well as) utter newness, to know
That somewhere close by or
Far away you share another's
Wakefulness, another human heart
And mind, another flat-backed
(Man, woman, child)
Staring skywards saying,
I think better in the dark.

Silence Streams

Like an aurora, silence streams across the sky,
And though I cannot see or touch it passing by,
And people say it's nothing, simply absent sound
My inward ear still hears and wonders why.

Silence can be golden, hold a precious hue.
Why not pink or purple, caramel or cobalt blue?
It is not one but many, and its spectrum loud and soft
Can fill a million galaxies and morning's drops of dew.

Gift your silence colour, play with rainbow light,
Gift your silence texture, weave it fine or tight,
Gift your silence freedom, let it wildly roam
And search for hidden spaces, where it will ignite

And touch the infinite. Let it the framèd portrait,
The unframed face, sun's rise and set, commemorate.
Release your silence to your senses; touch and
Hear its dormant seeds awake to green and propagate.

Yours Sincerely

for Helen Taylor Robinson

Grave Goods

Is a book
I never want
To finish,

And never will.
I read aloud
Pleased my voice
Did magnify

Your words
That were not words,
Portals rather,
Messengers from

The unseen,
The untouched,
The unimagined.
The soul's striations.

Like glaciers we
Descend life's valley,
Dissolve and are as one
In oceans' arms.

I, George Scrivens

If in some smothering dreams you too
…could hear, at every jolt, the blood
Come gargling from the froth-corrupted lungs…
My friend, you would not tell with such high zest
To children ardent for some desperate glory,
The old lie: *Dulce et decorum est*
*Pro patria mori.**
– Wilfred Owen

You, who think war glorious listen to my plea,
Who tell young men – *dulce et decorum est pro patria mori*,
Come to my Gethsemane and watch one hour with me.

For me there is no peaceful death, no churchyard eulogy,
In foreign mud and sludge and grime I'll die,
Tell me if war is glorious when you listen to my plea.

Shot and paralysed, alone in a deathly hole in deathly
No-man's-land no man hears my sigh. Please, by and by
Seek out my Gethsemane and watch one hour with me.

Through ten fevered days and icy nights my body
Sweats and shakes. Above the shells and bullets fly.
Is your war still glorious? Can you heed my plea?

Caked in mud and excrement the rats with me make free;
They drink my blood, my flesh they eat. Before I die
Lay down in my Gethsemane and watch one hour with me.

I see frail failing shadows; the boy I used to be,
I hear a song, a voice I knew – singing a lullaby.

Young men, for peace stand vigil. Heed his plea.
Remember his Gethsemane. Now, watch a while with me.

dulce et decorum est pro patria mori: It is sweet and right to die for your country. – Horace

George Scrivens, British army sergeant: shot in World War I at Arras on the Western Front, 21 May 1916. Found in a shell hole in no-man's-land on 31 May 1916. Dehydrated and rat-eaten, he had significant blood loss and raging septicaemia. He died at Aubigny-en-Artois 11 June 1916. He was 21.

At Ullamalla

i.m. Archie Macfarlane, ANZAC Day 2015

Old footprints lost, by memory were restored
In this the newest and the oldest land,
Where high above the wide-winged eagle soared,

Where a misty morning holds its own reward,
And sun sets golden with a crimson band.
Old footprints lost by memory were restored,

When we recalled his youth, how he explored
These valleys and these hills; the skies he scanned
Where high above the wide-winged eagle soared.

In the war to end all wars our youth were gored
In mud-filled trenches and on Gallipoli's sand
Many footprints were lost, never to be restored.

He returned to Ullamalla – his head was bowed,
His body broken. He could not lift his eyes and
Scan the skies where the wide-winged eagle soared.

The words 'No death in love that lives' are carved
On Archie's grave. With love we take a stand,
Promise footprints lost, by memory will be restored,
Recall how once he like the wide-winged eagle soared.

Hymn for Heaney

The weeks and months were moving past
And now the years are flowing too,
Birch, beech and alder leaves are falling fast,
We lift our eyes and turn our thoughts to you.

You laid down stepping stones for our comings
And our goings, sang hymns in praise of bogs
And sunsets, coal men and eel fishermen.
You led the long dead back to light, granted passage

Their epitaphs to write. Dig down, dig deep
Spread roots within well anchored words and
Like masted trees be firm to bend in stormy times.
You said all this, or words to this effect.

You taught us as you were taught – that mind is vast.
And you like Dante's Virgil our trusty guide, our how-to
Man, trowel-lifter, spade-wielder. Your poems your life outlast
Our hearts renew; fresh shoots our minds imbue.

Old Ground

He had no more need of days and weeks and months,
The particular year was of no account, and when asked
To name the prime minister of Australia he declined.
Mind you, these days that changed so often, if found
Not to know he would be forgiven and excused.

He stepped back from all these minor matters and retreated;
Not so much a retreat as a return. He had no need
For walls and doors; no love of the high-rise.
His was open ground (where anyone could come and go)
Ground that had since time immemorial been walked

Upon and watched over, tended and sown by poets.
Here once the spoken word had reigned supreme,
The music and the sight of sound repeated from
Generation to generation. Here words were first
Chiselled into rock. Here parchment and berry ink

Came into vogue. Manuscripts and books arrived,
And the printing presses, and then the internet.
He didn't care. They were all the same to him,
All means to an end. Surrounded by riches
Every morning he just sat and waited while

Seeds scattered by the world's poems germinated,
Sprouted, made flowers and leaves and branches
And full-grown trees. And when the sun danced
Upon his face or the moon silvered his already
Silver hair, or the wind blew louder and longer

Than had been foretold, or darkness removed all
Curves and lines and demarcations, it mattered
Not at all. And if he spoke little it was not he had
Nothing to say. He was past the waste of time.
He just waited. There was so much listening to do.

www.ingramcontent.com/pod-product-compliance
Lightning Source LLC
Chambersburg PA
CBHW062202100526
44589CB00014B/1915